BRICKS

Graham Rickard

Consultants: The Brick Development Association

Titles in this series

Bricks

Glass

Oil

Paper

Plastics

Steel

Water

Wood

Cover: (Main picture) A bricklayer building a wall. (Top right) A very old mausoleum in Central Asia, built of baked brick.

Editor: Sarah Doughty

First published in 1991 by
Wayland (Publishers) Ltd
61 Western Road, Hove
East Sussex, BN3 1JD, England

© Copyright 1991 Wayland (Publishers) Ltd

British Library Cataloguing in Publication Data
Rickard, Graham
 Bricks.—(Links)
 I. Title II. Series
 666

ISBN 0 7502 0158 4

Typeset by Dorchester Typesetting Group Ltd
Printed in Italy by G. Canale & C. S.p.A.
Bound in Belgium by Casterman S.A.

Contents

All the words that appear in **bold** are explained in the glossary on page 30.

What are bricks?

Bricks are small building blocks of clay or mud. They have been dried in the sun or baked in a **kiln** to make them hard and strong. Builders use bricks to make walls. To build a wall, builders lay bricks in lines, one on top of another, and stick them together with clay or **mortar**.

The size of bricks varies from one country to another, but most modern bricks are small enough to be held easily in one hand. Bricks are usually twice as long as their width – a standard brick measures 65 x 102 x 215 mm.

Above Bricks are commonly used to build modern cities such as New Delhi, India.

Right A modern brick, with a hollow, or 'frog' in the top.

4

There is often a hollow in the top surface of a brick. This hollow is called a 'frog'. The 'frog' is filled with mortar to help to make a stronger wall.

Millions of bricks are used all over the world every year. The USA alone produces about 6,500 million bricks in one year. Bricks can be made of different **materials** and used in many ways. This book looks at the many different kinds of bricks, and how they are made and used.

Bricks are made at a brickworks. Brickworks are usually found near building sites.

5

Why use bricks?

We all need buildings, as places where we can live, work and sleep in safety and comfort. Builders usually use whatever materials they can find locally for building. Stone and wood are often used, but they both have drawbacks. Stone buildings are very strong and last a long time, but stone is very heavy, expensive and can be difficult to work with. Wood is cheaper and easier to use, but it needs to be well looked-after to stop it from rotting.

A wooden building such as this house in Utah, USA, is easily damaged by storms and floods.

Many parts of the world do not have large supplies of stone or wood, but most places have plenty of clay or mud which can be used to make bricks. Bricks are useful because they are fairly easy to make and use, and are quite cheap to produce. They are also very strong, last a long time and can look very attractive.

Above *Patterns in bricks can make walls look attractive.*

Below *Bricks are useful because they can be cut and split in many ways.*

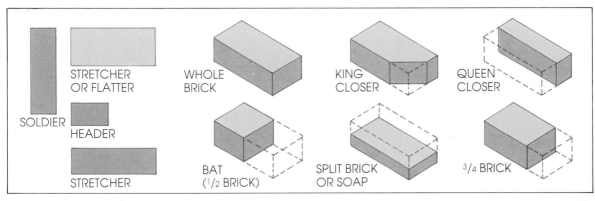

SOLDIER

STRETCHER OR FLATTER

HEADER

STRETCHER

WHOLE BRICK

BAT (1/2 BRICK)

KING CLOSER

SPLIT BRICK OR SOAP

QUEEN CLOSER

3/4 BRICK

The history of bricks

Bricks are one of the world's oldest building materials. The first bricks were made in the Middle East about 10,000 years ago, from the mud left behind after rivers had flooded. These bricks were moulded by hand into the shape of small French loaves of bread. They were left to dry in the sun, then stuck together with mud or **tar** to make walls. The ancient city of Ur, in modern Iraq, was built with mud bricks in about 4,000 BC.

The art of making bricks spread west from the Middle East towards Egypt. This wall engraving shows how the Ancient Egyptians made bricks.

Brickmakers soon found that they could make stronger bricks by burning them in a fire. The art of making these strong bricks then began to spread east and west.

8

The Great Fire of London destroyed the city's wooden buildings. They were replaced by stone and brick structures.

The Great Wall of China was built with bricks in 210 BC, and the Romans used bricks throughout their great Empire.

The Great Wall of China was built several thousand years ago. It is 2,400 km long and built of bricks.

Many of these brick buildings still stand today, as they are strong and fire-resistant. A few hundred years ago there were many terrible fires in European cities, such as the Great Fire of London in 1666. The cities burned because they were built of wood. They were then rebuilt with bricks to make them more fireproof. Bricks became more and more popular, and were used to build the new homes and factories that were needed during the **Industrial Revolution**.

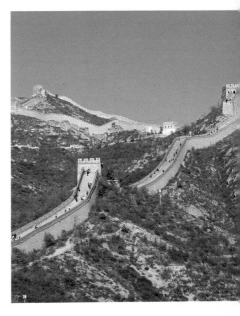

Mud bricks

Mud bricks are made from mud or clay, and simply left to dry in the sun. They are not as strong as bricks that have been fired in a kiln, but they are a very useful building material if they are kept dry.

In many countries, such as India and Malawi, the mud is pressed into **moulds** by hand, and is sometimes mixed with straw, animal hair or cow dung, to make the bricks stronger. The bricks are then stuck together with liquid mud or clay to build walls.

Mud bricks are made by hand and left to dry in the sun.

Arab builders use mud bricks to build thick walls, with tiny windows, to keep out the sun's heat. In Mexico, dried clay blocks are used to make **adobe** walls, and liquid clay is smeared on the outside to give a smooth surface. The roofs of some adobe houses hang out over the walls, to protect the walls from the rain.

Adobe houses in New Mexico, USA, are built with mud bricks and coated with liquid clay to give a smooth finish.

Digging clay

At one time, all the clay needed for making bricks was dug by hand, using spades to cut the clay into blocks. The clay was then taken to the brickworks by wheelbarrow or horse and cart. Clay is still dug by hand in some parts of the world, but it is very hard work because the clay is heavy, sticky and hard to dig.

Modern brickworks use so much clay that huge machines, such as diggers, bulldozers and scrapers are used in large clay pits. Sometimes a long chain of buckets, called a 'dragline', digs the clay from as deep as 20 m.

Big machines are used at clay pits for digging and moving clay.

The clay is then taken to the brickworks on a conveyor belt or in large dumper-trucks.

Restored clay pits have been made into lakes for leisure activities.

When a clay pit has been emptied of clay, it leaves a large ugly hole in the countryside. But old clay pits have several uses. Sometimes they are filled with rubbish, which is covered with soil and used for farming or growing trees. Otherwise they can be filled with water to make beautiful lakes.

Handmade bricks

All bricks used to be made by hand, and the art of making handmade bricks has not really changed for thousands of years.

First, the clay is crushed into small pieces and mixed with water until it is soft. The brickmaker then cuts off a lump of clay, rolls it in sand and pushes it firmly into a wooden mould, which has the 'frog' at the bottom.

Making bricks by hand, using a wooden mould.

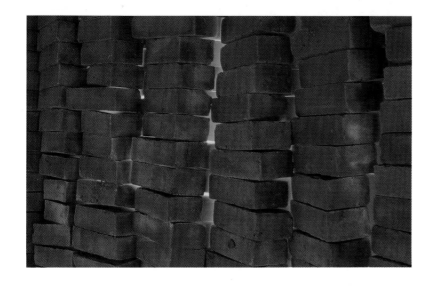

A stack of bricks is fired in a kiln to make the bricks harder and stronger.

If the brickmaker has used too much clay, he or she cuts it off by pulling a wire across the top of the mould. The brick is then tipped out of the mould and stacked in a drying room. Soft bricks are called 'green' bricks and take about a week to dry.

The bricks are then stacked in a kiln, which is like a large oven. They are fired for two or three days at over 500°C and then left to cool. Even a skilled brickmaker only makes between 800 and 1,000 a day. This means that handmade bricks are very expensive, but they are still used for special jobs, such as restoring old buildings.

Machine-made bricks

The first machines that made bricks were driven by steam, and the bricks were fired using wood or coal as fuel. Modern machinery is powered by electricity and gas to fire the kilns. Machine-made bricks are much quicker and cheaper to make than handmade bricks, and just a few people are needed to make many thousands of bricks a day.

This diagram shows how bricks are made by the process of extrusion.

There are several ways of making bricks by machine, but the most popular is by **extrusion** and wire cutting.

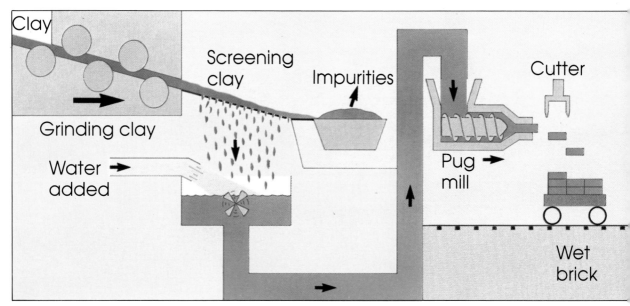

Clay

Grinding clay

Water added

Screening clay

Impurities

Cutter

Pug mill

Wet brick

To do this, the clay is ground and mixed and then forced, or extruded, through a machine. This makes a long square-shaped bar of stiff clay, which is then cut to exactly the right size by wire cutters.

The bricks are carried to the drying rooms, where they are placed in large racks for a few days. Then the bricks are put on to trucks which are pushed slowly through a tunnel kiln where they are fired and cooled. A modern kiln can take as many as 80,000 bricks at a time. The whole brickmaking process only takes eleven days.

Above Dried 'green' bricks are stacked in a kiln, ready for firing.

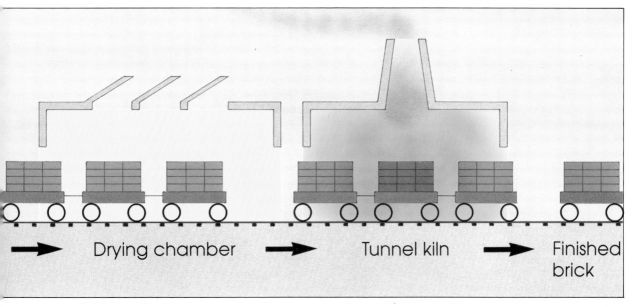

Drying chamber → Tunnel kiln → Finished brick

Transporting bricks

Stacks of bricks in a builder's yard, ready to be moved to a building site.

Large quantities of bricks are very heavy and difficult to transport. In the past there were many small brickworks, each one built near the town where the bricks were used. The only way of moving the bricks from the brickworks to the building site was by horse-drawn cart. In the eighteenth and nineteenth centuries, canal barges were often used for transporting bricks over longer distances. Later, trains and steam-powered lorries were used to do this, but the bricks still had to be loaded and unloaded by hand.

Large quantities of bricks can be moved quickly and easily with a fork-lift truck.

In a modern brickworks, the bricks are packed in parcels of about 500, wrapped in plastic, and strapped together with metal bands. All this is done by machine, saving a lot of time, effort and money. The bricks are then taken to the building site on a special truck. The truck has its own small crane on the back for lifting the packs of bricks on and off the truck.

A mobile crane is used to lift a stack of concrete blocks.

Building with bricks

Although bricks are now made and transported by machines, they still have to be laid by hand. Bricklaying is a very skilled job. A bricklayer builds a wall by placing the bricks on top of each other in layers, called **courses**. Using a pointed **trowel**, the bricklayer covers each course of bricks with a layer of mortar. This is a mixture of **cement**, sand and water. The mortar sticks the bricks together, and sets very hard when it is dry.

A bricklayer lays bricks in courses which are held together by mortar.

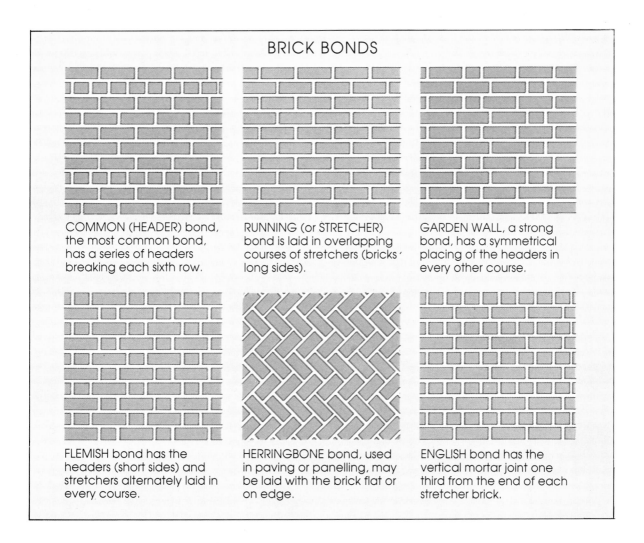

BRICK BONDS

COMMON (HEADER) bond, the most common bond, has a series of headers breaking each sixth row.

RUNNING (or STRETCHER) bond is laid in overlapping courses of stretchers (bricks' long sides).

GARDEN WALL, a strong bond, has a symmetrical placing of the headers in every other course.

FLEMISH bond has the headers (short sides) and stretchers alternately laid in every course.

HERRINGBONE bond, used in paving or panelling, may be laid with the brick flat or on edge.

ENGLISH bond has the vertical mortar joint one third from the end of each stretcher brick.

Bricklayers also use a **plumb line** and a **spirit level** to make sure that the brickwork is straight and level. The bricks are laid in patterns, called **bonds** to make sure that the vertical joins between each brick do not meet. If the bricks were simply stacked on top of each other in straight lines, the wall would be very weak and might soon fall over.

A diagram showing the different patterns or bonds that can be made with bricks.

Special bricks

Bricks come in many different sizes, shapes and colours, and they all have their own special uses. Firebricks, for example are made from a special clay and do not crack under intense heat. They are used to line fireplaces, kilns and furnaces.

These special bricks are used for making pavements in Saudi Arabia.

Engineering bricks are strong and hard. They are used to build walls which support the weight of heavy structures, like bridges.

Pavements and floors are made with bricks called 'pavers'. Stable 'pavers' are bricks that have grooves to provide extra grip for people to walk on and drainage to take away water from the pavement surface.

Not all bricks are made of clay. Some modern bricks are made of concrete, and others are made of sand and **lime**. Walls can also be made of glass bricks. This lets plenty of light into a building. Glass bricks are made in several different colours and are often used in office blocks.

Glass bricks are often used inside buildings to let in light.

Making concrete blocks

These concrete blocks have been made by hand. Liquid concrete is poured into moulds and allowed to set.

Concrete is a mixture of cement, water and stones. It dries out and sets to form a very hard building material. Concrete was first used by the Romans, and is still widely used in the modern building industry. To make concrete blocks, liquid concrete is poured into moulds and the concrete is allowed to set.

Builders laying courses of concrete blocks. Concrete blocks are quick and easy to build with.

Concrete blocks are much larger than bricks, and they are also cheaper because they do not need to be fired. They are not as strong as bricks, but are much easier and quicker to work with.

Modern buildings often have walls where the outer part of the wall is made of bricks and the inner part is made of concrete blocks. Between the two is an air gap, which helps to keep the building warm in winter and cool in summer. Modern lightweight concrete blocks can also be made by bubbling air through the concrete before it sets. These blocks provide good **insulation**.

Many modern walls have bricks on the outside and concrete blocks on the inside.

Making soil bricks

In developing countries, concrete and bricks are often expensive. Until recently some people in these countries had to rely on handmoulded mud bricks to build the new homes, schools and factories. Mud bricks, however, are not very strong, and are easily damaged by heavy rain.

A recent invention now allows people to make bricks quickly and cheaply. The invention is a simple hand-pressing machine, which uses a mixture of soil, water

This recently-invented block-making machine makes cheap bricks from a mixture of soil, water and cement.

and a small amount of cement (or lime). It is easy to use and produces strong soil blocks, which can be used in the same way as bricks. By using this machine, six people can produce sixty blocks an hour, and buildings made from the blocks will last up to thirty years.

This method has already been used to build new villages in Kenya, Nigeria and the Caribbean, and will soon be helping to build new homes in many other parts of the world.

These new houses in a village in Kenya were built with soil bricks.

Projects with bricks

Make your own bricks

You will need:

Plasticine in two colours
Matchboxes

A craft knife (with an adult's help)
A rolling pin

1. Push lumps of Plasticine of one colour firmly into the trays from the matchboxes to shape them. Then empty your Plasticine shapes on to a table.

2. Using a craft knife, cut each piece of Plasticine across its width into three equal pieces. These are your bricks.

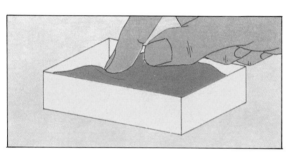

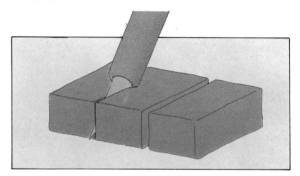

3. Using the other colour of Plasticine, roll it out into a thin sheet, and cut it into small pieces to fit between your bricks. This will be your mortar.

4. Use your Plasticine bricks and mortar to build a wall.

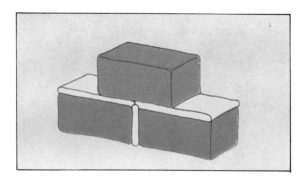

Try making the main patterns or bonds with your bricks. Turn to page 21 and try to follow the example of each bond shown.

Make a clay pot

You will need:

Pottery clay
A craft knife (with an adult's help)

A rolling pin
Water

1. Knead the clay until it is soft, and roll it out on a flat surface using a rolling pin.

2. When the clay is about 1 cm thick, cut out the base of your pot.

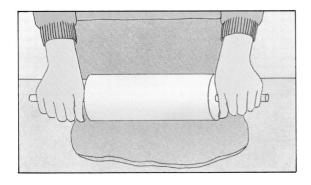

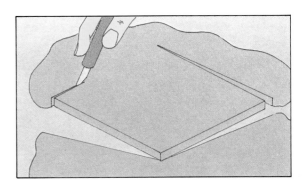

3. Cut out two sides the same length as the pot and stick on to the base using a little water.

4. Cut out the two pieces of clay to fit at the ends of your pot. Seal all the edges with water.

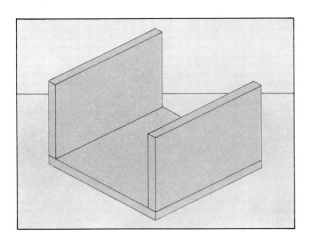

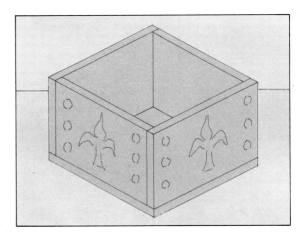

5. Cover your pot, and leave it for several days in a warm, airy place to dry.

If your school has a kiln, ask your teacher to fire your pot to make it stronger and longer-lasting.

Glossary

Adobe   Adobe walls are made of bricks of clay that are left to dry in the sun.

Bond   The pattern of bricks in a wall. The bricks are arranged to overlap to give the wall strength.

Cement   A fine, powdery material that sets hard when mixed with water.

Courses   Even, horizontal layers of bricks in a wall.

Extrusion   When a material is squeezed out of a machine to produce a particular shape.

Industrial Revolution   The period during the eighteenth and nineteenth centuries when industry and mechanization began to develop and expand.

Insulation   The prevention of heat loss or gain in a building.

Kiln   A large oven, used for firing bricks, pottery or glass.

Lime   A chemical found in certain rocks. It was originally used to make mortar before the invention of cement.

Material   A substance which can be used to make something.

Mortar   A mixture of cement, sand and water which is used to stick stones and bricks together.

Mould   A container which is used to give something a shape.

Plumb line   A piece of string with a weight on the lower end, which is used to check that something is vertical.

Spirit level   A tool used to check if a surface is level. It is usually a length of wood or metal, with an air bubble inside a sealed tube of fluid. When the bubble is in the middle of the tube, the surface is level.

Tar   A black sticky substance formed from coal, wood or peat.

Trowel   A flat, pointed triangular hand-tool, used by bricklayers to spread mortar.

Books to read

Arnold, H. **A Book about Bricks** (Macmillan, 1990)
Cash, T. **Bricks** (A & C Black, 1988)
Clarke, D. **How It's Built** (Marshall Cavendish, 1979)
Kurth, H. **Build a House** (Puffin, 1975)
Rickard, G. **Building Homes** (Wayland, 1988)
Rickard, G. **Focus on Building Materials** (Wayland, 1989)

Useful addresses

Australia
Brick and Pipe Industries Ltd
271 William Street
Melbourne
Victoria 3000

CSIRO Building Section
9 Queens Road
Melbourne
Victoria 3000

Sydney Building Information Service
525 Elizabeth Street
Sydney 2000

Canada
Clay Brick Association of Canada
1 Sparks Street
Ottowa
Ontario K1P 5A5

New Zealand
Building Research Association of
  New Zealand
290 Great South Road
Greenlane
Auckland

UK
The London Brick Company Ltd
Stewartby
Bedfordshire MK43 9LZ

The Building Centre
26 Stone Street
London WC1E 7BT

Brick Development Association
Woodside House
Winkfield
Windsor
Berks SL4 2DX

Acknowledgements

The author would like to thank Mr Ralph Knight and the London Brick Company Ltd for their help in compiling this book.

Index

Picture acknowledgements

The publishers would like to thank the following for allowing their photographs to be reproduced in this book: Building Research Establishment (David Webb) 26, 27; Cephas Picture Library (Mick Rock) 6, 14, 17, 18 (bottom); Chapel Studios (Zul Mukhida) *cover* (bottom), 7, 15, 20, 25 (bottom); C. M. Dixon *cover* (top); Mary Evans 8, 9, (top); Eye Ubiquitous (Paul Seheult) 4 (bottom), 19, 25 (top); the Hutchison Library *title page*, 10 (Chris Parker), 22 (Bernard Gerard); J Allen Cash Ltd 13; Panos Pictures 5 (Neil Cooper), 24 (Marc French); Photri 9 (bottom), 23; Graham Rickard 18 (top); Sefton Photo Library 12; Wayland Picture Library (Jimmy Holmes) 4 (top); Zefa Picture Library 11. All artwork is by Jenny Hughes.